Every Day

Perfectly Perplexing

© Waverley Abbey Resources 2021
Published 2021 by Waverley Abbey Resources. Waverley Abbey Resources
is an operating name of CWR, Waverley Abbey House, Waverley Lane,
Farnham, Surrey GU9 8EP, UK
Registered Charity No. 294387 Registered Limited Company No. 1990308

Unless otherwise indicated, all Scripture references are from The Holy Bible,
New International Version (Anglicised edition), copyright © 1979, 1984,
2011 by Biblica (formerly International Bible Society).
Concept development, editing, design and production by Waverley Abbey
Resources.
Front cover image: Adobe stock
Printed in the UK by Yeomans

[1] Anne Lamott, *Travelling Mercies*, (New York: Anchor Books, 2000)

[2] Donald McCullough, *The Trivialization of God: The Dangerous Illusion of a
Manageable Deity*, (Colorado Springs: NavPress, 1995)

[3] Donald McCullough, *The Trivialization of God: The Dangerous Illusion of a
Manageable Deity*, (Colorado Springs: NavPress, 1995), p. 41

[4] https://www.thegospelcoalition.org/video/

MIX
Paper from
responsible sources
FSC® C021017
www.fsc.org

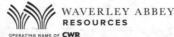

WAVERLEY ABBEY
RESOURCES
OPERATING NAME OF **CWR**

Letter to Readers

Dear readers

This is the last edition of *Life Every Day*, published by Waverley Abbey Trust.

Thank you for your readership of these notes over the years. We hope you have found them illuminating, encouraging, thought-provoking and uplifting. We pray that your walk with Christ has been rich, adventurous and intimate as you've journeyed with us in these notes.

We'd like to extend our thanks to Jeff Lucas for his faithful service in providing these notes for over 17 years. We are grateful for the thought, time and inspiration that he has poured into this publication.

Waverley Abbey Trust values the relationship with Jeff Lucas, which stretches back over many years. We have worked together on *Life Every Day*, but also on a myriad of books authored by Jeff and published by Waverley Abbey Trust and CWR. We've enjoyed his books, which are always insightful and challenging.

If you would like to stay up to date with Jeff's latest publications, or keep in touch with him, please visit his website, jefflucas.org. If you'd like to continue to receive Bible notes by Jeff, he is authoring a new range of notes, which you can find at lifewithlucas.co.uk

As Waverley Abbey Trust continue to educate and equip people for Christian service through *Every Day with Jesus* and *Inspiring Women Every Day*, together with an increased investment into its many online and face to face courses, we pray that Jeff's new initiative with Life With Lucas will continue to encourage God's people.

We hope you enjoy this final edition of *Life Every Day*.

With every blessing,

Mark Markiewicz
Chief Executive Officer
Waverley Abbey Trust

How to get the best out of *Life Every Day*

- Ideally, carve out a regular time and place each day, with as few distractions as possible. Ask God what He has to say to you.

- Read the Bible passages suggested in the 'Read' references. (As tempting as it is, try not to skip the Bible reading and get straight into the notes.)

- The 'FOCUS: ' reference then gives you one or two verses to look at in more detail. Consider what the reading is saying to you and what challenges that may bring.

- Each day's comments are part of an overall theme. Try to recall what you read the previous day so that you maintain a sense of continuity.

- Spend time thinking about how to apply what God has said to you. Ask Him to help you do this.

- Pray the prayer at the end as if it were your own. Perhaps add your own prayer in response to what you have read and been thinking about.

Join in the conversation on Facebook
facebook.com/jefflucasuk

Jesus behaving badly

Originally, I wanted to call this series of notes, 'Jesus behaving badly.' But then I was concerned that title was inappropriate, or even blasphemous. Let's be clear at the outset of our journey: Jesus was and is the only human being who has ever lived an utterly sinless life, and so there was never a second when He behaved 'badly'. Ponder that truth, and be amazed. There was never an episode of lust, jealousy, self-obsession, or corrupt motives. That doesn't mean Jesus didn't battle against temptation, because He was 'one who has been tempted in every way, just as we are, yet he did not sin' (Heb. 4:15). He faced the moral battles all human beings face, and triumphed.

Why does this truth matter? Christ's sinlessness is the key to His work of saving us, because He was the pure and perfect sacrifice, the Lamb without blemish, who died, not to save Himself, but to rescue us.

So why did I consider that title? It is because many events (including the manner of His birth, as we'll consider later) came as a total surprise. Jesus is exactly the One we need, but He often acts in ways we least expect. And again, as we'll see, the people who were most frequently shocked by Jesus were the religious elite who were convinced they knew the most about God and His ways. The Pharisees continuously suggested Jesus was behaving badly, being offended and frustrated by what He said and did. We begin our time together by celebrating the spotless, sinless Jesus.

Prayer: You are the spotless, pure Lamb of God, Lord Jesus, and yet You gave Yourself freely for Your world, and for me. I worship You. Amen.

Read:
Hebrews 7:26–28
1 Peter 2:22–25

FOCUS

'Such a high priest truly meets our need—one who is holy, blameless, pure, set apart from sinners, exalted above the heavens.' (Heb. 7:26)

He often acts in ways that we least expect

A terrible ambition

Read:
Genesis 3:1–24
Isaiah 14:1–15

FOCUS

'For God knows that when you eat from it your eyes will be opened, and you will be like God, knowing good and evil.'
(Gen. 3:5)

It's been said that God made humanity in His image, and ever since the Fall, humanity has been trying to return the favour. In trying to understand why some thought Jesus' behaviour was puzzling and even out of order, we need to look further back in history, to the beginning in Eden. All was as it should be: that's what made Paradise so wonderful. God and His creation, humanity, were in harmony, and the partnership the Lord always intended was functioning well. Adam was invited to name the species, and then he and Eve were given the responsibility of stewarding the good earth God had made. Everything the first couple needed was wonderfully provided, and they lived freely, with just one prohibition: don't eat the fruit of one designated tree.

Then the whispering began, and as Satan began to accuse God, the alluring possibility was offered: you can be like God Himself, on equal terms, no longer subjects. This speaks to the central nature of what sin is, the desire to be like God, if only in our own lives, as we are tempted to become the captains of our own souls, as William Henley put it in his poem, 'Invictus'. This also shows us the desire to have a God of our own liking and choosing is rooted deeply in us all. Satan convinced Eve that the boundaries God had set were wrong – and therefore, in a sense, God was behaving badly. But His way is right, and His character holy and blameless. Let's trust Him and what He says.

His character holy and blameless

Prayer: When I am tempted to try to make You into what I want You to be, quickly show me my error, Lord. You are God. Amen.

Let's make a god we like

W̶e see a deep-rooted desire to be god-like when we look at the story of the Exodus and those wandering souls, the people of Israel. God had stunned them with His amazing power, rescuing them from the mighty pursuing Egyptian army. But how quickly we forget, and how impatient we can be. Weary of waiting for Moses to return to them, they rushed into making an idol and worshipping it. Their actions were ludicrous: they affirmed that Moses had been the agent of their deliverance, yet they quickly dismissed his importance. They then constructed something of their own making to provide for their future protection. Depraved behaviour resulted – it often does when we drift into vague spirituality that promises religious experiences but makes no moral demands. Aaron then seemed reluctant to take responsibility for his lax leadership. He admitted to allowing an offering of gold, but then suggested a golden calf just jumped out of the flames! It's easy for us to fall into the same sin, but in a much more subtle way. Let's ponder Anne Lamott's warning: 'You can safely assume that you've created God in your own image when it turns out that God hates all the same people you do. [1] Ouch!

Notice that it was God's own people, those saved from Egypt, who fell into this sin. We can falsely presume that because we too find ourselves among the saved ones, we are impervious to this temptation. But, as we'll see, nothing could be further from the truth.

Prayer: I want to be like You, Lord, in Your beautiful character, and never attempt to make You like me. Save me when that temptation comes. Amen.

Read:
Exodus 32:1–35
Acts 7:39–43

FOCUS

'Come, make us gods who will go before us. As for this fellow Moses who brought us up out of Egypt, we don't know what has happened to him.' (Exod. 32:1)

God had stunned them with His amazing power

Revision not abandonment

Read:
Exodus 32:1–8
1 Kings 12:25–30

FOCUS

'These are your gods, Israel, who brought you up out of Egypt.'
(Exod. 32:8)

As we look again at the disastrous choices those ancient Israelites made, it's important to see that they didn't outrightly reject God, at least in their own thinking. Their sin was rather more subtle, because they chose to *amend* Him. As they made their calf, they immediately paid homage to it as the god that had rescued them (which was ridiculous because they had only just made the calf). Humans often pretend their behaviour is wise, when in fact it's folly. To put it another more biblical way, professing ourselves to be wise, we become fools. The Israelites wanted a god who would rescue them from their enemies, but not one who would lead them into a wilderness. In the days to come, we'll consider some of the golden calves we can make, but for now, why don't we ask the Holy Spirit to show us where we might have formed an image of God that is more to our liking than to His revelation in Scripture?

The subtitle for Donald McCullough's brilliant and deeply challenging book, *The Trivialization of God*, is 'The dangerous illusion of a manageable deity.'[2] Perhaps that last sentence cuts right to the heart of everything: we want a God who can help us, but One we can manage; a Saviour, a blesser, a provider, but not a Lord and master. We don't reject Jesus; we just reshape who and what He can be. I'm deeply challenged to search my heart and ponder my decisions in the light of that uncomfortable reality. How about you?

we want a God who can help us, but One we can manage

Prayer: I tremble at the thought that I could be tempted to amend You to fit in with my own preferences and requirements. Save me from that, Lord Jesus. Amen.

The divine supermarket

Read:
Mark 8:27–30
John 14:1–7

FOCUS

*'But what about you?'
he asked. 'Who do
you say I am?'
(Mark 8:29)*

During the trips my wife Kay and I lead to the Holy Land, we often visit the amazing ancient site of Caesarea Philippi. There you'll find the ruins of an ancient temple site which the guides like to refer to as the 'supermarket of the gods': a place where you could worship the god of your choice. One of the most popular choices was Pan, the god of fear – from whom we get our word 'panic'. But if Pan didn't help you out, you could just make another selection. At the site is a cave, known in ancient times as 'The gate of hell', and in that cave is a rock, where perhaps human sacrifices were offered. It's amazing that Jesus took His disciples to this very location to put the vital question to them: 'Who do you say that I am?' He also used the site as a visual aid to His teaching, affirming that Peter would preach a rock of truth, and 'the gates of hell' wouldn't be able to overcome that truth – His authority and power were over all. In a supermarket of idols, He was nudging them to see empty shelves, and place Him alone as the Son of the Living God.

At a time when vague spirituality is in fashion, we live in a supermarket of gods too, and the temptation is to believe following any of them will lead us to a rock-like foundation of truth for our lives. But Jesus claims exclusivity, and He calls us to make our choice about Him, not once, but daily, as we determine to follow Him. Let's choose well.

Prayer: Today, I affirm, You are the Lord, the Christ, my Lord, my God, my King, Jesus. Amen.

Jesus claims exclusivity

Read:
Matthew 11:1–19
Matthew 9:9–13

Those who try to control Jesus frustrate Him

During parties, I dread party games. When I'm asked to act something out, participate in charades, or otherwise do something that usually ends up with me looking like a complete fool, I want to run and hide. I think it's the challenge of not being in control of what happens.

Jesus uses an illustration of spoiled children, upset when others don't want to participate in their games by dancing on cue when the music plays for a wedding game, or wailing on demand when a funeral game (weird!) was played. Jesus addresses how people make demands, complain when they are disappointed, and can't be pleased. They are equally irritated by the ascetic tendencies of John the Baptist as they are with Jesus' gregarious habit of eating and drinking with sinners. His critics were like petulant children, and in their pickiness and critical attitude, they missed the wisdom of God, the Messiah Himself. Let's not try to revise God, or resist Him because we're disappointed that He won't dance to our tune.

To ponder: Have you ever tried to make God 'dance to your tune?' What happened?

Weekend

Let's not try to revise God

Fervently religious but deluded

When it comes to which group repeatedly claimed Jesus was behaving in a puzzling or even bad way, the Pharisees top the list. When we read the gospels, it seems they followed Him around, just waiting to catch Him doing something they could criticise, and they were very vocal in their complaints. We'll return to them later, but for now, let's see that these men viewed themselves as *the* experts in religion in general and holiness in particular. A lay people movement formed 200 years before Christ, the name *Pharisee* means 'the separate ones.' When a man became a Pharisee, he first endured a probationary period up to a year in length, during which time he had to prove his ability to keep the rituals of the Law, and so these religious barons were great lovers of Scripture. They placed a strong emphasis on prayer, often devoting three hours daily to it. Unlike the Sadducees, they were hoping the Messiah would come, and they believed in the supernatural, in the resurrection of the body, in judgment after death, and in angels and demons. Unlike the Zealots, they were committed – at least in their theology – to peace and non-violence. But these fastidiously religious idealists became some of Jesus' bitterest enemies. Passion, intense spirituality and theological orthodoxy don't guarantee we will completely grasp what Jesus is doing. In fact, we might even become His fiercest critics. Let's be aware.

Read:
Luke 11:37–53
Matthew 23:1–12

FOCUS

'The Pharisees and the teachers of the law began to oppose him fiercely and to besiege him with questions, waiting to catch him in something he might say.' (Luke 11:53–54)

we might even become His fiercest critics

Prayer: When I feel convinced I am so right, but miss the point and even call what You are doing wrong, open my heart and my eyes, Lord. Amen.

Humility and mystery

Read:
Isaiah 40:1–26
Job 8:1–11

FOCUS

'Who can fathom the Spirit of the LORD, or instruct the LORD as his counsellor?'
(Isa. 40:13)

In a while we will begin to look at some episodes where Jesus acted in a totally puzzling way. But permit me a word of caution before we do. I don't want us to feel we can totally explain everything Jesus did, or for us to rush to hasty conclusions. And while I do want us to understand Him, I don't want us to try to defend Him. In the early days of my Christian journey, I rapidly concluded I had God figured out, and I couldn't have been more wrong.

Four decades later, there are many things I don't understand about how God works and why He does (and does not) do certain things. I'm more at home with mystery. I now see the confession, 'I don't know' is not a cop-out, but a simple acceptance of the fact that I stand as a mere human being before the unfathomable mightiness of God. To trust without fully understanding is often not an indication of a lack of faith or an unwillingness to dig deep: it can be a stance of unwavering faithfulness. I've certainly seen this countless times as a pastor, watching helplessly as people who love God have suffered horrendous pain but have refused to loosen their grip on Him by faith. In my eyes, they are heroes. And so, when we get to each difficult episode, let's not make another golden calf, which is the god of our understanding – a concept we'll consider more later. The god that we completely comprehend is no god at all. As we recognise that, we may not have all the answers, but we can have peace.

I don't understand about how God works

Prayer: I bow humbly before You, Lord, and submit myself to what I know of You, trusting in the vastness of what I neither know nor understand. Amen.

Bringing this home to us

Yesterday we paused and considered the need for humility in the face of mystery. Let's pause again today and ask Jesus to do nothing less than shake us up and even disturb us. How easy it is to settle into a vague, comfortable faith that cheers us up but never challenges us, that comforts but never brings about real heart change. I mentioned Donald McCullough's book, *The Trivialization of God*, earlier. I'm deeply challenged by his words, even if they might be a little overstated: 'When we stay focused on the Jesus of Nazareth revealed in the New Testament, we discover no "gentle Jesus, meek and mild", but One who grabs us by the scruff of the neck to shake loose from us all false images of deity we have cherished, One who is the great iconoclast smashing to bits our trivial gods.'

In fact, there is a beautiful, gentle side of the Jesus who does invite us to come to Him as weary souls because He is gentle of heart. Our problem comes when we will only let Him be the gentle, tender Shepherd, and we baulk at the Jesus who flipped tables over in the Temple courts, or we ignore His blunt rebuke of Peter, advising the hapless fisherman to 'Get behind me' and tagging him as Satan. Or we cheer as we read how Jesus spoke such scathing words of rebuke to the Pharisees, but never consider that He might blast *us* for some of the meaningless and irrelevant buffoonery that we Christians can indulge in. Let's count ourselves in for renewed challenge.

Prayer: Stir me, where I have become complacent; unsettle me, where I have become satisfied with less than Your best, Lord Jesus. Amen.

Read:
Mark 11:15–19
John 2:13–17

FOCUS

'He overturned the tables of the moneychangers and the benches of those selling doves.'
(Mark 11:15)

He might blast *us*

The Jesus who supports my cause

Read:
1 Corinthians
12:27–31
Romans 12:3–8

....

FOCUS

'Are all apostles? Are all prophets? Are all teachers? Do all work miracles? Do all have gifts of healing? Do all speak in tongues? Do all interpret?'
(1 Cor. 12:29–30)

The man was passionate and angry. Utterly committed to his cause (I won't identify it here because it isn't the point) he rightly pointed to many scriptures that proved his concerns were biblical. God cared about what he cared about, he insisted. But we can end up thinking that our particular concern is *all* that God cares about. We can end up only listening to voices that support our view. Our reading of Scripture then becomes selective, and we focus on the passages that endorse our passion, ignoring other concerns. So instead of serving God by working for a just cause, we end up serving a just cause by using God.

Within the local church community, this will cause tension. We can become focused with a relentless drive to elevate our causes, and we denigrate the passions of others. The worship leader looks down on the social activist as being not spiritual enough: the social activist sneers at the worship leader, seeing them as having their head in the clouds. Both are dismissed by the evangelist who thinks care for the poor and worship are secondary: when are we going to get out and tell people about Jesus? Our gifts and passions become weapons. Let's embrace godly causes, but don't make gods out of them, and let's treat those who feel differently with respect. We are a body, with different roles. So let's act cooperatively and acknowledge that while what we care about may be important, not everyone needs to share our level of concern.

Prayer: May my place in church balance my passion, patient when vision seems unreachable, kind when my concerns get lost, respectful of others' burdens. Amen.

Our gifts
and passions
become
weapons

The Jesus who is in line with what my crowd thinks

FOCUS

'Fools find no pleasure in understanding but delight in airing their own opinions.'
(Prov. 18:2)

Becoming involved in Spring Harvest, the European teaching and worship gathering, was one of the greatest learning experiences of my life. I discovered wonderful Christians, quite unlike me in their worship styles and theological convictions. One of the beautiful aspects of the Church is its diversity. Unity is not about uniformity. While we need to agree on the essential foundations of the gospel, we interpret what the Bible has to say about a wide variety of issues differently. It's good to have confidence about what we believe but, as we saw yesterday, that can too quickly morph into a superior attitude, where we sneer at those who don't believe exactly what we believe. We think we have God all figured out. We then gravitate to reading books and attending conferences, written or arranged by people who share our views. Both the books and the conferences simply endorse our convictions. We start to think of ourselves as defenders of the truth: our group alone is right. So how can we avoid this downward spiral? One antidote is simple humility: be willing to listen to dissonant voices. This is not in order to win the argument, or to listen for 30 seconds before moving on: this is in order to learn, to understand and to interrogate what we think. Truth needs to be defended but not with a defensive attitude. Our confidence is in Scripture, but we can be too eager to think that our understanding of Scripture is the only one that is right.

Prayer: Lord, grant me the humility to allow what I believe to be examined, courage to stand for truth, and wisdom to be teachable. Amen.

Our confidence is in Scripture

WEEKEND 13/14 NOV

The Jesus as I perceive Him

Weekend

If you've been a Christian for a while, you will have formed a perception about what Jesus is like – unique to you. Our perception of God is not downloaded in a pure, consistent form, but is the result of countless sermons, hymns, conversations with other Christians, and the books we've read and conferences we've attended, as we saw yesterday. Our view of God is also shaped by our life experience, our parents, and the influence of Christian leaders we have encountered. We don't have a perfect understanding of Jesus: our perception of Him is like a patchwork quilt. But we still tend to think our view of Him is accurate. We all need to face the fact this is not the case: that's what the life of faith entails. One day, we will see Him face to face, and the eternal experience of discovering His currently unfathomable character and heart will continue without our current blurred vision. But acknowledging that our view of Him is at best incomplete is vital. Now, 'we know in part'.

To ponder: Do you agree that our perception of Him is like a patchwork quilt, and we tend to think our view of Him is accurate?

We don't have a perfect understanding of Jesus

The Jesus who wants me to be comfortable

Read:
Luke 9:57–62
Matthew 16:24–28

FOCUS

'Jesus replied, "No one who puts a hand to the plough and looks back is fit for service in the kingdom of God."'
(Luke 9:62)

It's a question rightly asked by many churches who seek to serve their communities – what are the 'felt needs' of people, and how can we respond to those needs? And that's a great question to ask. But caution is needed, because while the gospel is a call to live life as it was always intended to be, arm in arm with God by faith – it is not a message designed to help us to be happier. Princeton psychologist Robert Wuthnow said: 'Spirituality no longer is true or good because it meets absolute standards of truth or goodness, but because it helps me to get along. If it helps me find a vacant parking space, I know my spirituality is on the right track. If it leads me into the wilderness, calling me to face dangers I would rather not deal with at all, then it is a form of spirituality I am unlikely to choose. [3]

The heart of the gospel message is both the cross and the resurrection. Jesus invited a number of Galileans to journey with Him in the most impactful, exciting journey in history, but one that would cost most of them their lives. Their response led them on a painful and, at times, bewildering journey. An over-sentimental and misguided view that says, 'God is love and loves me, therefore He only wants me to be comfortable' will lead us to feel that, when the road is tough and the calling hard, Jesus is not being faithful. But while God does want to comfort us when life is painful, He never promised us a life of comfort.

Prayer: Wherever You lead me, Lord, I want to be faithful as a follower. Strengthen and enable me by Your Spirit. Amen.

He never promised us a life of comfort.

It's goodbye... and perhaps, hello

I've been privileged to have written daily Bible reading notes for 17 years now. *Life Every Day*, published by CWR/Waverley Abbey Resources, impacted thousands of readers, and demanded that I write over a million and a half words - a tall order!

When the new leadership at Waverley decided to go in another direction, Kay and I really thought this aspect of our ministry, Bible note writing was at an end - and we were quite wrong. Hundreds of readers made contact asking that there be a continuation of notes in some form.

And so we are delighted to announce that an exciting new daily Bible reading note product - *Life with Lucas* - has been birthed, a publishing endeavour produced by our ministry. The new product will be available from January 1st 2022, so if you are a *Life Every Day* reader, that will cease publication on December 31st 2021- there's no need to miss a beat! We're grateful to the leadership at Waverley Abbey Trust for the opportunity to share this news with you all.

Available by annual subscription or directly through the many wonderful Christian retailers in the UK, the plan is to take bible reading notes to a whole new level, with links to podcasts, online video introductions to each set of notes, free linked resources for small groups, and an online 'going deeper' section as well. The notes will be published on a quarterly basis.

Quite apart from the demand from readers, which has been so encouraging, I'm thrilled to be developing this new project because we so need the truth of God's word applied in our lives daily. We've spent a long time in a variety of lockdowns - and through all of that I've come to realise that much of the

Bible was written by people in lockdown, for people in lockdown! Whether it's the Israelites enslaved in Egypt, Joseph falsely accused and incarcerated, Daniel and his friends exiled in Babylon, Paul, the apostle who wrote his amazing prison epistles, or John, trapped on the prison island of Patmos - the Bible speaks so directly to the challenges that have become so pressing for the world recently.

The notes will be Christ centered - at least one month in each edition will focus on the Gospels, as well as offering a balanced diet of themes and doctrinal exploration. In full colour throughout, the hope is that *Life with Lucas* will be lively, attractive, and loaded with great content, humour and authenticity.

Finally, I want to offer huge thanks to you, the readers - some of you have been with us from the very beginning. It has been a great joy to meet you as Kay and I have trekked around the country, and many of you have been kind enough to offer encouragement and feedback through letters, email and on social media.

To find out more about the new product or to subscribe, go to **lifewithlucas.co.uk**

The Jesus who makes me successful

Read:
2 Peter 2:1–19
Philippians 4:11–13

FOCUS

'These teachers will exploit you with fabricated stories. Their condemnation has long been hanging over them, and their destruction has not been sleeping.' (2 Pet. 2:3)

I've often written, both in *Life Every Day* and elsewhere, about the damage that has been done by the prosperity/health and wealth movement within the global church. I risk the ire of some readers in speaking out as I have, but, as we saw yesterday, the promise that following Jesus (and giving large amounts of money to TV evangelists) guarantees financial riches and success in life is completely untrue. It also creates a superficial view of what real prosperity is. Many of those who spend their lives frantically climbing the ladder of success end up emotionally fractured as they haul themselves up to another level. Arriving at a level of so-called success, they continue onward and upward, hungry for more, and hoping they will find some peace and satisfaction. Like a donkey endlessly following that carrot on a stick but never getting to enjoy snacking on it, we continue on our never-ending pursuit of the next thing; the bigger, the better.

I wonder how many, who once bought into the prosperity gospel message, are now no longer following Jesus, because the false promises failed them? They may think that Jesus let them down, even though He ended His life poor and powerless, as we know.

It's wonderful to be able to enjoy some good things in life, and to be competent in what we do. But ultimately, success is not measured by accumulation and status, but by faithfulness, deep friendship, service and love for God and commitment to His purposes.

success is not measured by accumulation

Prayer: Grant me true prosperity, Father: joy, relationships, and most of all, knowledge of and love for You. Amen.

The Jesus who loves my nation

I live much of the time in America, where I am currently classified as a 'resident alien', which means that I can be legally live and work there. If Kay and I were to become citizens of the USA, we would technically have dual citizenship in both the USA and the UK (while paying taxes in both countries!) But actually, we would have no less than three 'citizenships', because our primary identity is as citizens of the kingdom of God. Writing to the Philippians, who lived in a Roman colony and were proud of their Roman citizenship, the apostle Paul reminded them where their greatest allegiance should lie. But our priorities as Christians can get tangled. When Donald McCullough was a pastor, he removed the American flag from the platform of the church building, and it caused quite a stir.

Jesus constantly upset and disappointed people, because while He came first to the people of Israel – more about that later – He came for the whole world. Those who wanted Him to be a political Messiah who would kick the Romans out and restore Israel's fortunes were frustrated when, instead of doing so, He allowed Himself to be arrested and ultimately executed by them. I love my British heritage, and the opportunity to live in America. But first and foremost, my call is to the kingdom. While true patriotism, which includes serving and praying for a nation, is good; nationalism, which usually includes a sense of superiority, is certainly not.

Prayer: When my allegiance to You conflicts with my allegiance to any earthly nation, help me to choose You and Your kingdom values, Jesus. Amen.

Read:
Philippians 3:17–21
Ephesians 2:11–22

FOCUS
'But our citizenship is in heaven.'
(Phil. 3:20)

my call is to
the kingdom

The Jesus who always says yes

Read:
Matthew 16:21–28
Matthew 20:20–28

....

FOCUS

'Jesus... said to Peter, "Get behind me, Satan! You are a stumbling block to me; you do not have in mind the concerns of God, but merely human concerns."'
(Matt. 16:23)

Remember those nodding dogs that used to adorn the back shelves of cars? The motion of the moving vehicle caused the pivoted head of the plastic dog to move up and down, giving the impression this particular artificial canine was always in agreement with whatever was going on. Rover always said yes (especially if it was in a Rover... sorry!)

It might seem inappropriate to use the nodding dog to criticise the idea of a nodding Jesus who is always in agreement with whatever we want to do, but the absurdity of the illustration serves its purpose. It's clear Jesus often said no when his friends and disciples came up with bright ideas. As we have seen, Peter's suggestion that Jesus should not go the cross was met with a stinging rebuke which included the words, 'Get behind me, Satan.' The two sons of thunder, eager to call down fire and brimstone on an unreceptive Samaritan village, got a firm 'No' (Luke 9:55). And speaking of those two brothers, when their mother, Salome, put in a request that her boys enjoy the best seats of power and influence in what she saw as the coming kingdom, she was firmly refused. The Jesus who always smilingly says 'Yes' is a product of our imaginations. Jesus is not a genie who exists to rescue us from our own disastrous choices. Because He loves us and knows best, He will sometimes prohibit rather than permit. When was the last time he said 'No', to you, and how did you respond?

Jesus is not a genie

Prayer: I love you, Lord, and want to obey You. Enable me to be faithful when my desires pull me in a direction You don't want for me. Amen.

The Jesus who always says no

Let's consider the thought, looked at earlier, that Jesus always says 'No', especially when we're asking Him about something we really love and cherish. In my first faltering steps as a Christian, desperate to know what God's will for my life was, I got very confused. I think I actually came close to a nervous breakdown. Someone very unhelpfully advised me the will of God is generally what we don't want to do, which really caused some consternation. Perhaps you've heard similar advice: 'Don't tell God that you'd rather not be a missionary, because if He hears you say that, that's where you'll end up.' For me, the confusion was about marriage rather than vocational calling. Engaged to a beautiful girl called Kay, I assumed that Jesus' verdict on our relationship would be a thumbs down, (because I loved her and marriage was what I wanted) and that, to follow that dysfunctional advice, I needed to marry someone whom I didn't want to marry, if I was to win His approval. That warped view nearly cost me the marriage that I've been so grateful for these last 42 years, which would have been a tragedy. I've come to believe, as we delight ourselves in the Lord, He shapes our hearts and loves to give us what we desire. He doesn't always say 'Yes', but often He does – and His 'No' is because He loves and wants the best for us, even though there may be circumstances in which we never understand why He has done so.

Read:
Psalm 37:1–40
Matthew 6:33

FOCUS

'Take delight in the Lord, and he will give you the desires of your heart.'
(Psa. 37:4)

Prayer: Your plans for me are good, Lord. Help me to rest in the times when You say 'Yes', and be obedient when Your call is a loving 'No.' Amen.

we delight ourselves in the Lord

The Jesus who is a muscly macho man

Weekend

As a child, I used to enjoy watching Saturday afternoon wrestling on television. My auntie Hetty was a big fan, and I'd curl on the couch with her, and we'd yell at the television together. Muscle-bound hulks with names like Jackie Pallo, Big Daddy, Mick McManus and Giant Haystacks (whose real name was Shirley) would threaten and growl at each other before the match.

Some Christians, in an attempt to make Jesus more palatable to men in what they see as a feminised culture, have tried to portray Him as the ultimate 'man's man'. This has led to some very silly talk: one well known speaker complained we have 'recast Jesus as a limp-wrist hippie in a dress with a lot of product in his hair, who drank decaf and made pithy Zen statements about life while shopping for the perfect pair of shoes.' He went on to say, 'I cannot worship a guy I can beat up.' But the Jesus of the Bible was tender, gentle, able to weep, and called for His friends to support Him in Gethsemane. No macho image needed.

To ponder: What does Jesus teach us about true masculinity?

the Jesus of the Bible was
tender, gentle, able to weep

The Jesus who is the fourth emergency service

Read:
Mark 12:28–30
Hebrews 12:1–3

FOCUS

'Love the Lord your God with all your heart and with all your soul and with all your mind and with all your strength.'
(Mark 12:30)

In case of an emergency, we have an alarm system in our home which includes a panic button. One press of it will summon the police, an ambulance or the fire brigade – helpfully we can select which one so all three don't show up at once. Having that facility gives us a sense of security, knowing help would be at hand, hopefully quickly, if necessary. Many view Jesus in the same way, as a last resort: a handy first responder available on call when life gets rough, but one we needn't be concerned with when all is going well. Thousands will pray '999' prayers, (911 in America) today, desperate for God's help. They won't, however, want to have an ongoing relationship with Jesus, or they will not realise a friendship with Him is available. C.S. Lewis remarked, 'We regard God as an airman regards his parachute; it's there for emergencies—but he hopes he'll never have to use it.'

But this is not just a malady afflicting non-Christians. I confess that, when challenging circumstances come (as has happened recently with some health concerns within our immediate family), my prayer life suddenly livened up and became more urgent. Perhaps that's natural, but let's always remember God does not just want to help and bless us in extreme situations. He wants to walk with us as we follow Him by faith. I'm so thankful I can call upon Him in the wintry season when fears stalk me, but I want to know Him and walk with Him in the summer seasons too.

Prayer: Faithful God, help me to walk with You through all of life, and not just call upon You when times are hard. Amen.

He wants to walk with us

The Jesus who is just like us

Read:
Psalm 89:1–8
Psalm 71:19

FOCUS

'Who is like you, LORD God Almighty? You, LORD, are mighty, and your faithfulness surrounds you.'
(Psa. 89: 8)

One of the more subtle ways in which we try to make Jesus conform to being the Saviour who is to our liking is simply to imagine Him to be just like us. So if you visit a church in China, you might see a picture of Jesus that portrays Him as Asian. In the Western world, we have our own Scandinavian-looking Jesus, with flowing blond hair and piercing blue eyes. In an African-American church, you might see a black Jesus. Even though each is a false representation, because Jesus was a near-Eastern Jew with olive skin, perhaps these are attempts to show the human Jesus who identifies with us, and us with Him. It doesn't matter what Jesus looked like – the fact is, in coming to our planet, He identifies with every one of us.

Jesus is utterly like us in His humanity, yet utterly unlike us in His sinlessness and His divinity. There's a famous song that asks the question, what would happen if God was simply one of us? But He is not just one of us. He came among us, but He is totally unlike any other there has ever been, both in His unfailing love and His total holiness. The word 'holy' means 'to be marked off from the ordinary' – here is no God to be rationalised or dumbed down. Some writers have called this quality of holiness 'the great stranger', so utterly unique is it in the universe. His purity is perfect, His power beyond understanding, He is 'the beautiful One' (Psa. 27:4). The holiness of God means that in no sense is God one of us.

He is not just one of us

Prayer: There is none like You, holy, mighty, loving God. I worship You. Amen.

The Jesus who has a side that I like

When we're talking about aspects of someone's character, we often refer to their 'side'. 'I know he can be awkward, but he has a very caring side to him.' If we're trying to be gracious, we focus on their positive side, and if we're looking for fuel for criticism, we give attention to the side we dislike.

We can shape our own view of Jesus by only focusing on certain sides of Him, even as we read Scripture. We love the stories where He blessed children, ate with sinners, and told off the religious villains of the day, those Pharisees. We even cheer when He turns over the tables in the Temple courts. But we can be less inclined to ponder the Jesus who insists we die to ourselves, deal absolutely ruthlessly with lust, or adopt the attitude of a servant. We edit Him subtly, like the crowds who loved Him because He provided wine for a wedding, or loaves and fish for many thousands. John Piper has challenging words of warning: 'He is the Jesus of the Bible, or he's the Jesus of your imagination. If he's the Jesus of the Bible, you take the whole Jesus. You can't carve him up in pieces. The whole Jesus is the Jesus who loves the church. He died for the church. [4]

As one who longs to see people experience the forgiveness, grace and love of God, I realise I can easily slip into this tendency. How about you – do you love a particular side to Jesus, but ignore another one?

Read:
John 6:16–59
Matthew 12:38–39

FOCUS

'Jesus answered, "Very truly I tell you, you are looking for me not because you saw the signs I performed but because you ate the loaves and had your fill."' (John 6:26)

Prayer: I want all of You, Lord, not just the 'side' of You that I prefer. Amen.

You can't carve him up in pieces

The Jesus who is a New Age guru

Read:
John 14:1–14
John 6:60–71

FOCUS

'Jesus answered, "I am the way and the truth and the life. No one comes to the Father except through me."'
(John 14:6)

Browsing in a huge bookstore recently, I was struck by the number of self-help books available, many of them 'spiritual' in content. A quick survey revealed that most authors were pointing their readers to a happier, healthier, more fulfilled life. The number of titles showed that countless different pathways were available – the idea was to pick one of them and see if it worked. Sometimes Jesus appeared as a candidate to lead us to a 'higher consciousness'. Popular New Age author Deepak Chopra, speculating about the years between Jesus' childhood and His adult ministry, suggests Jesus found spiritual enlightenment as a result of bumping into a wise sage on an icy mountaintop – and now Jesus can help us, regardless of our religious traditions. But Jesus is far more than an advisor; He casts Himself as the ultimate authority and the only pathway to salvation, forgiveness and transformation. He is *the* way, not *a* way. His claims were shocking, and led to His crucifixion. As we turn to look now at episodes where Jesus' behaviour seems difficult to understand, let's affirm once again that He is the Christ, and, with the disciples, we have nowhere else to go apart from Him. Most of them died martyrs' deaths because of their utter conviction that He was not only who He said he was, but He had also beaten the powers of death and hell. We need more than a coach. We need a Saviour, and that rescuer is Christ alone.

He is *the* way, not *a* way

Prayer: You are the Christ, the Son of the Living God, the Way, the One with the words of eternal life, Lord Jesus. Amen.

Jesus – a racist?

Read:
Genesis 11:1–9
Galatians 3:26–28

FOCUS

*'Then they said,
"Come, let us build
ourselves a city, with
a tower that reaches
to the heavens, so
that we may make a
name for ourselves."'*
(Gen. 11:4)

The tragedy of George Floyd's death stirred the hearts of millions across the planet. It goes without saying (but let's be clear) that all racism, be it personal or institutional, is not just morally wrong but is an affront to God. His heart has always been to see the walls of prejudice collapse, that all humans live peaceably and respectfully. All injustice angers the God who has such a broken heart for the oppressed. But before we look at controversial episode in Jesus' ministry, one that, at first glance, could give the impression that He was endorsing the cultural racism of His day, let's know that racism is not new. Instead, it is rooted in the very heart of who we are as fallen human beings. Racism is fuelled by a sense of superiority (the idea that we are better) and confirmation bias (we look for evidence to support our prejudice, and ignore anything that contradicts our false ideas). When we look at the story of building of the tower of Babel, we see not only total rebellion against God, but pride too – 'we may make a name for ourselves'. My point is this: while we need social reforms, justice for the oppressed, institutional and cultural renewal, we also come back to the ultimate answer, which is Jesus – salvation through Christ Himself. The history of the cancer of racism is long, and its source runs deep, to the human heart. The gospel is not just good news, but vital news, and it speaks to the enduring curse of racial injustice.

Prayer: Search my heart, O God, and reveal any hidden hints of racism in me. In Jesus' name, Amen.

a broken
heart for the
oppressed

Read:
John 4:1–9
John 8:48

WEEKEND 27/28 NOV

Racism and the culture in Jesus' day

In Jesus' day, racial tension was everywhere, although it tended to centre more around ethnicity than skin colour. The Greeks despised the Persians, calling them 'barbarians'. Mary Beard, professor of Classics at Cambridge, said, 'The Greeks painted a contemptuous picture of the Persians as trousered, decadent softies who wore far too much perfume. Then the Romans came along and, minus the trousers, said much the same about the Greeks.'

And Jews saw themselves as superior. Instead of being a beacon people for the whole world, they became arrogant, even cursing other nations. They called the Gentiles 'dogs', and viewed themselves as the true Jews. As for the Samaritans, they had built a rival temple on Mount Gerazim (and intermarried with other races), so the Jews wrote them off as 'half breeds'. The worst insult was to call a Jew a Samaritan (John 8:48).

Jesus grew up in that culture of racial hatred. Did that kind of thinking shape Him in any way?

To ponder: Cultural views about racism have changed a lot in recent years. Has culture imbedded any racial stereotyping in you?

racial tension was everywhere

The problem

Read:
Matthew 15:21–26
Mark 7:24–30

FOCUS

'He replied, "It is not right to take the children's bread and toss it to the dogs."'
(Matt. 15:26)

The man sniffed. 'All that stuff you said in the sermon about interpreting Scripture carefully, Jeff. I don't buy that. I just take Scripture at face value.' I gently explained that taking Scripture seriously is not the same as taking it all literally. Jesus is the Lamb of God, but that doesn't mean that He's a sheep. We're told that if our eye offends us, we should pluck it out, but kindly step away from the knife. There are many other examples I could offer, but just take a superficial look at this story. A Gentile woman comes to Jesus, begging for help for her demon-possessed daughter. The disciples bristle, wanting Jesus to send her packing. Jesus then calls the woman a dog – sorry, there's no way around this, that's what He said. He then enters into a debate with the lady, one that He loses, and then He heals her daughter. But this name-calling is profoundly disturbing. Jesus seems to be endorsing Jewish prejudice. It appears that He's being rude and insulting, which worries us, not least because He had just been teaching about being careful over what comes out of our mouths. Some commentators try to wriggle out of this, suggesting that, as Jesus used a soft word for dogs which means 'little dog', perhaps He was being playfully affectionate. To me, a dog is a dog. So what's going on? We'll ponder that tomorrow, but let's know now that Scripture deserves careful, thoughtful reading. It's a sword and, in the wrong hands, can do great damage.

Prayer: Enable me to handle Your Word correctly, Father, lest great damage be done. Amen.

Scripture deserves careful, thoughtful reading

Leading questions

Read:
Matthew 15:21–24
Luke 18:19

....

FOCUS

'He answered, "I was sent only to the lost sheep of Israel."'
(Matt. 15:24)

A man approached a rabbi and asked, 'Tell me, why do you rabbis always answer questions with a question?' The rabbi paused for a moment. 'So what's wrong with a question?' Think about it...

Jesus often used questions as teaching opportunities, to provoke others to think and debate. In the gospels, He asks 307 questions. One example is found in the encounter with the couple on the Emmaus road on Easter Day. Jesus not only acts as if He was heading further onward on the road (thus prompting an invitation to supper) but also gives the impression that He was unaware of what had happened in Jerusalem over the Passover period! All of this was to enable the couple to express their feelings and disappointment. More of that incident later...

The comment that Jesus posed to this woman was a leading one, prompting her to respond to the currently popular Jewish idea that the Gentiles were outsiders (dogs were roaming scavengers, not household pets). Teachers often use this as a method of exploring an idea: present it, and then allow the class to interrogate it. And Jesus always won debates, even with highly skilled experts in the law. But here, remarkably, He 'loses' the argument with a foreigner, and a woman at that (woman were not considered competent to debate the Law). Surely Jesus was leading her, and His listening disciples, down a pathway to thoughtful learning. What truths is He currently nudging us to understand in our own lives?

Jesus
often used
questions

Prayer: Lead to wisdom and truth, Lord, and may my questions – and Yours – be stepping stones to my understanding. Amen.

WAVERLEY ABBEY TRUST

Every day with
Jesus

These bimonthly Bible reading notes will bring revelation and encouragement to you in your walk with God. Written by Micha Jazz, they cover topics relevant to everyday life as a follower of Jesus. Each day has a reading, reflection, something to consider, a prayer to make and an action to take.

Inspiring
Women

Written by women for women, these popular Bible reading notes speak encouragement and wisdom into day-to-day life and all it entails. Be strengthened, challenged and empowered each day

We've got podcasts, emails, printed notes, online plans and much more.

waverleyabbeytrust.org

WAVERLEY ABBEY
COLLEGE

Higher Education at Waverley Abbey College
Be transformed through learning

Our part-time programmes equip you with skills and knowledge to release your God-given potential to operate in roles that help people.

We currently have two faculties that provide vocational training in Counselling and Spiritual Formation. Plus, our Leadership faculty opens in January 2022.

To find out more and apply, visit
waverleyabbeycollege.ac.uk

Or join us for an Open Day in November. Sign up on
waverleyabbeycollege.ac.uk/open-days

WAVERLEY ABBEY
COLLEGE

Higher Education Programmes

Spiritual Formation Faculty

MA Spiritual Formation

PG Dip Spiritual Formation

PG Cert

- Chaplaincy
- Mentoring and Coaching
- Pastoral Care
- Spiritual Direction

BA (Hons) Top-up

EMCC
European Mentoring &
Coaching Council

QAA Reviewed
Quality Assurance Agency
for Higher Education

Counselling Faculty

MA Therapeutic Counselling and
Psychotherapy

MA Counselling

BA (Hons) Counselling

Dip HE in Counselling

Leadership Faculty

MA in Public Leadership*

Dip HE Intergrating Faith and
Leadership*

*These programme are subject to validation
Launching in January 2022
Distance learning programmes*

We also offer Continuing Professional Development short courses in Spiritual
Formation and Counselling, including Counselling Supervision training.

To find out more call **01252 784731**
or visit **waverleyabbeycollege.ac.uk**
or email **admissions@waverleyabbeycollege.ac.uk**

Invest in Your Mental Health and Wellbeing

Explore our NEW *Insight Learning* online courses

Our Insight range lifts the lid and gives understanding into some key issues that many people struggle with. Drawing on biblical wisdom and professional expertise, our range of resources will help those facing challenges and those seeking to support others.

Now, adding to the Insight resources of books and devotionals, we are pleased to have launched Insight Learning, a series of courses available online.

In these video-based, online courses you can learn at your own pace and gain greater knowledge to better understand yourself and others. You have the choice to learn on an individual basis or you can sign up as a group.

Courses currently available:

- An Insight into Self-Esteem
- An Insight into Anxiety

To find out more and to sign up, visit
waverleyabbeyresources.org/insight

GIFT VOUCHER

Now Available

WAVERLEY ABBEY
RESOURCES

You can grab your gift voucher from our website, and let your friends / family choose their own treat from our vast array of Christian resources.

Choose from £10, £20 and £50 vouchers

£10

£20

£50

Buy your gift voucher here

www.waverleyabbeyresources.org/all-products

More clues

FOCUS

'He answered, "I was sent only to the lost sheep of Israel."'
(Matt. 15:24)

There's another clue showing Jesus was trying to expose the racial superiority of His disciples, rather than endorse it and reject the woman. It is found in His statement that He was only sent to the lost house of Israel – which was not true at all. Rather, He was sent *first* to Israel, but then to the world. Jesus *did* take His message to Israel first, initially telling His disciples not to visit Gentile or Samaritan villages with the good news (Matt. 15:21). This was not exclusivist or selective, but was rather the fulfilment of a promise and part of God's strategy. Abraham had been assured he and his family would be a vehicle of blessing to all of the earth (Gen. 12), after God disinherited all the nations following the rebellion of the tower of Babel. Now, the expectation was the gospel would come through the beacon people of Israel, in the coming of their Messiah. The vision of people from every tribe, tongue and nation being included in God's blessing (Rev. 10:7–9, Col. 3:9) would come as the Jews welcomed their Messiah, which again is why the apostle Paul went first to the synagogue in every city that he preached in. In talking with this woman as He did, Jesus was holding up the erroneous idea that God was only interested in Israel, exposing it in the unfolding conversation, and then confirming the truth of His inclusivity, both by healing her daughter and celebrating her faith. God keeps His promises – and works to a plan.

God keeps
His promises

Prayer: Lord, thank You for the promises in Your Word. Help me to live in the good of them, especially when life is hard. Amen.

Anger about exclusion

While staying focused on this controversial episode where the 'dog word' was used, let's widen our view for a moment by looking at one of my favourite episodes in Scripture – the turning over of the tables in the Temple courts. As we hear Jesus talk about the Temple being turned into a den of thieves, we could come to the conclusion that His radical act was simply about exploitation. It is true the worshippers were being ripped off by unscrupulous traders. But Mark's Gospel gives us further insight, saying God's intention for the Temple was that it be a 'house of prayer for all nations' – and the traders were gathered in the court of the Gentiles, the Gentiles' only access to the Temple area. The tables were blocking the way to God's presence, something that angered Jesus. It caused him to rebuke the Pharisees, because they put obstacles in people's way, burdening them with a heavy load of senseless rules.

The Church has often 'blocked the way' to those hungry to know God. When a local church becomes a club for a certain type of person, or a poor example of how to handle disagreement, when leaders morph into dictators, or prey on those who should feel safe, when preaching becomes irrelevant, or prayer becomes a tired old routine, the way is blocked.

Let's remember too that as Jesus refers to His Father's house, He is reminding us of the truth that the Church does not belong to us, but to Him. If He wants to topple some of our tables, let Him do so.

Prayer: I pray for the church I belong to, Father. May we be an open door, and never an obstacle to those who would want to know You. Amen.

Read:
Mark 11:15–18
Matthew 23:1–14

....

FOCUS

'And as he taught them, he said, "Is it not written: 'My house will be called a house of prayer for all nations'?"'
(Mark 11:17)

the Church does not belong to us

Who let the dogs out?

Read:
1 Timothy 1:12–17
Luke 15:1–2

FOCUS

'Here is a trustworthy saying that deserves full acceptance: Christ Jesus came into the world to save sinners—of whom I am the worst.' (1 Tim. 1:15)

Over the years, I have taken a fair amount of criticism for things I've written and preached, some of it well-deserved. But on one occasion, the heat was really turned up. It all happened when Rolf Harris was found guilty and sentenced to prison for his sexual offences. In a response on social media, I unreservedly condemned his behaviour, asked for prayer for his victims, and then requested prayer for him as well. I was hoping that, in a place of disgrace and aloneness, he would experience true repentance, grace and wholeness. That's when the barrage of criticism began. Some suggested I had no right to ask for prayer for Harris because of the nature of his crimes. One person said I must be a useless father and grandfather to request such a thing. But then I look at Scripture, and see a murderer of Christians, Saul, called and equipped to become the great apostle Paul. He continued to call himself the 'chief of sinners'. And it's very clear that Jesus spent much of His time not just preaching to, but eating and drinking with people whom society had completely written off, like tax collectors. The popular view was they could never find forgiveness even if they were repentant. We too can be tempted to write some people off as 'dogs', beyond the scope of love and grace, and the thought of them being forgiven is repellent to us. Are we guilty of deciding what is the unforgivable sin, and who, in our minds, should be left out in the kennel?

We too can be tempted to write some people off

Prayer: You reached out to the untouchables, Lord. Show me how to show outrageous grace, passing on the love You have shown me. Amen.

Read:
Matthew 15:21–24
Luke 18:1–8

The tenacity of faith

Before we leave this episode, let's focus on the Samaritan woman, because Jesus marvelled at the greatness of her faith. That's the kind of faith I'd like to experience in my own walk with God. First, she showed great insight as she called Jesus the 'Son of David', the Jewish title for Messiah, one which even the disciples themselves were only gradually coming to associate with Him. Obviously, the Holy Spirit had been at work in her life, granting her revelation and understanding. But she was also tenacious to the point of being irritating, and had caused the disciples to request Jesus to send her packing because of her shouting. Her sheer persistence is admirable.

Recently I have found myself in a situation where my prayers have not been very lucid, but they have been extensive. I have simply cried out repeatedly to God for His help, sometimes through the night, when fear looms largest. We can be weary of well doing and repeated praying, but there are times when we just have to keep on keeping on.

To ponder: Have you given up praying about an issue in your life, because of what seems to be a lack of response from God?

Jesus marvelled at the greatness of her faith

A strange encounter on the road

Read:
Luke 24:13–16
Luke 24:1–8

FOCUS

'Now that same day two of them were going to a village called Emmaus, about seven miles from Jerusalem.'
(Luke 24:13)

As we turn to an episode that happened on Easter Day (odd, I know, as we approach Christmas), we meet a couple taking a long journey home after the bewildering events of that Passover weekend. Jesus was alive, but they didn't know it and, as we'll see, utter despair was the result. As we continue to think about the Jesus who was puzzling at times, we'll identify a few strange aspects to this story. First of all, He doesn't introduce Himself to them, but pretends to be a fellow pilgrim heading home after the Passover. And then, He asks them about the events of the weekend, as if He didn't know every detail. The mysterious behaviour continues as He makes it look as if He is heading on to some further destination – what kind of game is He playing? And then, as they realise who He is, He immediately disappears – puzzling stuff indeed. We'll look closer at these details over the next few days, but for now, look at what can happen to us when it seems Jesus is dead. Be challenged along with me, because there are times when I respond to the difficulties of life without applying the truth that there is a God, He is all-powerful, and He is able to intervene. To put it bluntly, Jesus is alive, but in my responses and attitudes, He might as well be dead. My faith affirmations on Sunday morning don't seem to impact the issues I face on Monday. If Jesus is truly alive, however, everything may not be easy to understand, but it is different.

Jesus is alive

Prayer: May the reality of your triumphant resurrection impact my challenges and struggles, Lord Jesus Christ. Amen.

Paralysed by sadness

Perhaps we all arrive, at some point in life, at a place of exhaustion. We're so utterly shell-shocked, so bewildered by sudden, awful circumstances, that we hardly have energy to put one foot in front of the other. We just want to lie on the floor, and surrender to the crushing weight.

These two on the road to Emmaus were trudging along, so disappointed because Jesus had not turned out to be the military Messiah that, as good Jews, they had anticipated. They'd so wanted him to ride on the colt into Jerusalem and somehow overthrow the Romans, and establish a new government. Instead He'd turned the tables over in the Temple courts, but then allowed Himself to fall into the hands of the oppressors, and been executed. Maybe this couple had heard rumours of the resurrection, but obviously they had not believed them, and they spoke of Jesus in the past tense, as one now dead. And so now this is what they say to Jesus: 'We had hoped...' Sometimes that's the only prayer we can pray. It's generally thought they were supernaturally prevented by God from recognising Jesus – but a close study of the Greek doesn't make this clear. The text literally says their eyes were 'under arrest' or 'in custody' –the same word used to describe the arrest of Jesus. Perhaps it was tiredness, disappointment, unbelief, preoccupation with just getting home: we don't know. Today, whatever we feel or don't feel, we affirm that not only is He risen, but He is with us by His Spirit.

Prayer: Lord, may I find You there, when I am battling against disappointment. Amen.

Read:
Luke 24:13–17
Psalm 119:25–28

FOCUS
'They stood still, their faces downcast.'
(Luke 24:17)

'We had hoped...'

Learning in the journey 1

Read:
Luke 24:17–25
Isaiah 30:21

FOCUS
'"What things?" he asked.' (Luke 24:19)

Yesterday we considered the overwhelming sadness felt by the two on the Emmaus road. But here's a puzzling question: seeing their agony, why didn't Jesus immediately identify Himself, sweeping their pain away in a stunning moment of self-disclosure? When I'm in pain, that's the kind of response I want from God: instant relief, a clear voice in my ear, insight downloaded from heaven at warp speed.

Over the next few days, we'll explore the fact that Jesus wanted them to go with Him on a journey, not just to Emmaus and to supper, but to wisdom and understanding, as they trekked that shadowy road.

The first step on that journey of discovering came, not from listening to Jesus, but by pouring out their hearts to Him. He obviously knew all that had occurred in Jerusalem, but wanted them to express what they felt and how they understood it. Sometimes I can be tempted to ignore the discipline of prayer, because it feels as though I am blethering on to God about things that He already knows anyway – which of course He does. But as we talk out what is on our hearts and minds, we have the opportunity to consider the accuracy of our perceptions in His presence. And as we see Jesus gently rebuking the Emmaus pair, we stand open to His correction too. Sometimes, even as I pray, I see the folly of my thoughts even as I speak them out. Tell God what You think and feel, even if Your words are tinged with disappointment and even anger. He won't mind.

Jesus wanted them to go with Him on a journey

Prayer: Help me to share what is on my heart with You, Lord. Where I am wrong, show me. Amen.

Learning in the journey 2

Over the years that I've been writing *Life Every Day*, I have repeatedly stated, perhaps to the surprise of some of my readers, that these Bible notes are *not enough* to sustain you in your walk with Jesus. Hardly a good marketing comment, is it? But it's true. I'm grateful for the opportunity to share these reflections and prayers, and genuinely hope you find them helpful, but in today's complex world, where too many Christians barely know their Bibles, there is a need for us to dig deep, to gather helpful information and secure a strong foundation for our faith. In what must have been one of the greatest teaching events in history, Jesus revealed His identity by referring the bewildered couple back to the revelation of Scripture, specifically Scripture that pointed to Him as Messiah. Their understanding was not just rooted in the incredible experience of the risen Christ appearing to them, but what He taught them from the Word of God.

There was one specific error in their minds that needed correction: the relationship between the Messiah and suffering. Like Peter earlier, the thought of a crucified rescuer was quite beyond them; surely strength would characterise the Messiah, not the utter desolation and weakness of a man on a cross.

As we draw towards the end of another year, let's commit afresh to be people who wrestle with and imbibe God's Word, because in a turbulent world, it's our only sure foundation.

Prayer: Your Word, O Lord, is a lamp to my feet. Enable me to study it, reflect on and apply it, with the help of Your Holy Spirit. Amen.

Read:
Luke 24:25–27
2 Timothy 3:16–17

FOCUS

'And beginning with Moses and all the Prophets, he explained to them what was said in all the Scriptures concerning himself.'
(Luke 24:27)

these Bible notes are *not enough* to sustain you

Learning in the journey 3

Read:
Luke 24:25–27
1 Peter 1:3–9

FOCUS
'Did not the Messiah have to suffer these things and then enter his glory?'
(Luke 24:26)

Yesterday we saw the Emmaus pair struggling with the idea of a suffering Messiah. I don't want to move on too quickly from that thought because, put bluntly, many of us followers of Jesus also bristle at the idea that suffering can be part of our journey with Christ. We can live with the simplistic idea that if God is all-powerful, then He can shield us from suffering. So, when He doesn't, anger and resentment builds. But that is quite unfair. As we have seen, God has not promised us a blue-sky existence: in fact, He actually informs us that, this side of eternity, we will have trouble. The experience of Jesus and His disciples provide us with many obvious examples of faith leading to suffering, pain and death, rather than preventing it.

The truth that suffering will come is perhaps easy to embrace – until suffering actually arrives. It's then that, even if we understand, theologically, we are not spared struggle, we still instinctively want God to remove it. Like children who want a good parent to make their bruises better, we acknowledge we will experience hurt, but want it to go away anyway.

Readers often contact me with questions, feedback or prayer requests and, as I type these words, I know full well some of you are holding on to faith and faithfulness even though life, and God with it, are both quite puzzling right now. May you know grace and strength to journey along the dim pathway another day today.

God has not promised us a blue-sky existence

Prayer: May faith arise when life hurts most, Father. Amen.

Read:
Luke 24:28–31
Revelation 3:20

Learning in the journey 4

This part of the episode is really puzzling! First of all, the resurrected Jesus seems to be playing a joke on His friends, asking them to tell Him about everything when He already knows all the details. And then, He pretends to go further when they arrived home – the Greek wording makes it clear He has no intention of proceeding further, but wants them to have that impression. So what's going on?

I suggest that Jesus wanted the Emmaus pair to have the opportunity to invite Him in for supper. Some of us think that because God is the ultimate authority, He simply does what He wants, when and how He wants. But Jesus waits to be wanted. He invites us to invite Him into our lives, and seeks to draw everyone into relationship with Him. He never forces Himself on us. We are invited to choose whom we will serve. I love how the Emmaus two insisted He have supper with them – the word used doesn't mean a casual invitation, but a firm insistence. Let's tell Jesus that we insist on His presence today.

To ponder: How do you respond to the suggestion that Jesus waits to be wanted?

Jesus waits to be wanted

Join Jeff and Kay on a very special tour of Israel and Jordan. Previous tour members have commented that the tour was life changing - walking in the landscape of the Bible is an incredible experience!

Sharing their biblical insights and supported by expert local guides, with bluetooth headsets (in Israel) to make sure that you don't miss any of the enlightening commentary, Jeff and Kay will take you to the famous sites, including Galilee, Jerusalem and Petra.

The tour will visit some key biblical locations where Jesus walked like Capernaum, (His home base after He was rejected at Nazareth, an amazing site where you can see the remains of what was thought to be Simon Peter's house), the Mount of Beatitudes, where the greatest sermon of all time was delivered, enjoy a boat ride across the Sea of Galilee, the place where Jesus walked on the water and calmed the storm, the beach at Tabgha, where breakfast was shared with the bewildered disciples after the resurrection, and a walk down the Mount of Olives - the so-called 'Palm Sunday' route that Jesus took will lead us to the quiet and twisted trees of the Garden of Gethsemane - the place of such struggle and surrender. We also plan a visit to the baptismal site where Jesus was immersed in the River Jordan, with an opportunity for our guests to be baptized or celebrate their baptismal vows. We will also have an opportunity to float in the Dead Sea, the lowest place on earth. This is of course entirely optional, as is the head to foot coating of Dead Sea mud that you can enjoy as it is widely celebrated for it's anti-aging benefits!

Add to this our visit to the Western or 'Wailing' wall, the temple steps that led into the courts where Jesus turned the tables, literally, on those ancient rogue traders, and the Garden Tomb area - one of two sites where it is thought that

Jesus was buried. Of course, we celebrate the truth that He only borrowed the tomb for the weekend!

Another highlight will be our visit to Neot Kedumin Biblical Gardens, the Biblical Landscape Reserve in Israel, which is located halfway between Jerusalem and Tel Aviv. This unique recreation of the physical setting of the Bible in all its depth and detail allows visitors to see life as it was lived by our ancestors 3,000 years ago.

We will also cross the border into the nation of Jordan, and visit the spectacular city of Petra, and ride on jeeps across the amazing desert landscape of Wadi Rum, with its idyllic orange sands and rock formations. All this and so much more!

Our hotels are four star, with fabulous food, and include a stay in a 'kibbutz' hotel in Galilee - a Jewish community that has extended its work into the hospitality sector. We tour on an air-conditioned Mercedes bus, equipped with wifi.

Previous guests have shared about how such a wonderful sense of community is created during these trips, and we laugh, cry, learn and reflect together in what is definitely an unforgettable experience, and one not to be missed. We end most days with an optional evening gathering to reminisce and share together, hosted by Jeff and Kay. Of course, you may choose to opt out of that in order to enjoy a quiet refreshment in the hotel bar or get some additional sleep!

Book now for this amazing opportunity! Dates: 4th - 12th May 2022
For more information, prices etc visit: **www.toursforchristians.com**
Email: groups@travelinkuk.com Tel: 020 8931 8811

Learning in the journey 5

Read:
Luke 24:28–30
Proverbs 3:5–6

....

FOCUS

'When he was at the table with them, he took bread, gave thanks, broke it and began to give it to them.' (Luke 24:30)

Luke focuses repeatedly on how Jesus revealed truth as He shared meals, and the wording here obviously points us to the breaking of bread that we share in Communion, or the Eucharist. When I gather together with God's people to participate in the beautiful drama of taking bread and wine, I am gently drawn back into what is really true: the core of what it means to be human: knowing God and being loved and led by Him. But commentators also point out that Jesus was discovered by these two in the ordinariness of a shared meal. Coming to a table for food is something that we all, if we are blessed to live in the plenty of the developed world, do two or three times a day. Apart from those times of special celebrations and treats, sharing a meal is a very functional, everyday activity. There is a danger that we designate encounters with God as only being possible in sacred spaces, at events and religious conferences, whereas we can meet Him in the ordinary, the predictable, even the mundane.

That happened to me today. A close and dear friend (who would not consider himself to be especially spiritual) called me – just at the right moment when I needed his wisdom and insight. Knowing nothing of a situation that I'm currently navigating, he spoke right into my circumstances, even though he was quite unaware he was doing so. I ended the call, and then wept with gratitude, because in the ordinary, I had bumped into Jesus. Look out for Him.

knowing God and being loved and led by Him

Prayer: Meet me in the place of gathered worship; meet me in my work, my play, my laughter, my tears. Amen.

Learning in the journey 6

Read:
Luke 24:30–32
1 John 3:1–3

FOCUS

'Then their eyes were opened and they recognised him, and he disappeared from their sight.'
(Luke 24:31)

Commentators debate exactly what happened as Jesus suddenly disappeared. Some insist this was a miraculous and sudden event (and I share this view), while others want to say Jesus simply withdrew, allowing the pair to reflect on all they had seen and heard. What is clear is Jesus was no longer visible, which might have been frustrating. These two surely had so many more questions, and would have wanted to spend more time basking in the wonder of this shared meal. Instead, however, they were thrust back to the place of faith, where we all live with God as our priority even though He is currently invisible.

Not being able to see, touch, and often hear Him can get wearing, but this would be the way things would be, once Jesus had ascended. As a preacher, standing up week after week, feeling like I have a bucket of seed in my hand, throwing it everywhere and hoping it will bear good fruit, I often feel as though I'm investing in the invisible (often I can't see visible results) in the service of the invisible God. No wonder Scripture celebrates the truth that eternity will be about seeing Jesus face to face –the glory of heaven. The wonder there will not be about angel song or the death of death, or even being reunited with those who have gone before, glorious though all those things will be. It will be about seeing the One whom we currently are not able to see. As the old hymn says, what a day of rejoicing that will be.

Prayer: I have not seen, but I believe, and You call me blessed. I trust You, Lord. Amen.

we all live
with God as
our priority

Learning in the journey 7

Read:
Luke 24: 33–49
1 Corinthians
1:26–31

....

FOCUS

'They got up and returned... to Jerusalem. There they found the Eleven and those with them... saying, "It is true! The Lord has risen and has appeared to Simon."'
(Luke 24:33–34)

I n leaving, Jesus was entrusting the most important mission of all time to His friends. He was going away, and handing over the responsibility for getting the good news to the world to a select group of friends and followers. But these are not elite troops. There's those two on the road to Emmaus. I love the thought that even as they were trekking in entirely the wrong direction, Jesus walked with them. As soon as they realised the wonderful truth, they turned around and headed back to Jerusalem immediately. That pictures encourages me. Even when we get off the right path, we're not deserted. That doesn't give us a licence to wander, but is of special encouragement to those of us who love someone who is currently living the life of a prodigal, marching or drifting away from God. Whatever road they are on, God is out there, and can meet them. And then there's the picture of the gathered disciples back in Jerusalem. The resurrection did not answer every question for them – in fact, it created many more. As Jesus appears to them, they think they're seeing a ghost, they are startled and frightened, they doubt. He had to eat food to prove that He really was not just a spirit, and still they were unsure. Only after a little post-resurrection Bible teaching did the truth start to fully settle in their hearts.

Far from being superheroes, these were profoundly ordinary people called to be game changers for the world. Nothing has changed.

we're not
deserted

Prayer: In my weakness, my fragility, be my strength, that Your glory might be seen. Amen.

The biggest question in life

Recently an article appeared in INC magazine, exploring the most important questions of life. The list included asking if we're living by our values, what it is that we fear most, how we are taking care of ourselves, who are our friends, and what do we need to find forgiveness for – all vital questions. But as we consider the context of this strange episode, (which is really important if we are to understand it) we discover Jesus' disciples asked what is surely *the* most important question of them all.

Jesus and His disciples were crossing the Sea of Galilee, which can erupt suddenly in the most violent storms. As a visitor to Israel, I have talked with locals who have seen them. As Jesus calms the storm, He is fulfilling a role only God can fulfil in Old Testament thinking. The psalmist speaks of the One who can tame the waves. This was not just about controlling the weather. In ancient times, people viewed the sea as a place of chaos and even evil, which is why Jesus 'rebuked' the storm.

And so the sea crossing served as an opportunity for the disciples to see Jesus' mighty power at work, as the One with authority over sickness and the cosmos. The teaching session would continue because they are about to see that He has power over demons as well. But in the midst of this they ask: 'Who is this?' That is the single most vital question in life is: 'Who is Jesus?' The answer to that question is the beginning of everything.

Prayer: My trust is in You, Almighty God, risen Christ, ascended Lord. Amen.

Read:
Mark 4:35–41
Psalm 107:23–29

FOCUS
'They were terrified and asked each other, "Who is this? Even the wind and the waves obey him!"' (Mark 4:41)

Jesus' mighty power at work

What do we love?

Read:
Mark 5:1–20
Luke 14:1–6

FOCUS

'He gave them permission, and the impure spirits came out and went into the pigs. The herd... rushed down the steep bank into the lake and were drowned.'
(Mark 5:13)

A walk along a beach with two friends, Chris and his dog Barley, taught me that passionate animal lovers are everywhere. Chris is a friendly chap, but we were stopped every fifty metres or so by people who wanted to pet Barley, to find out how old he was, what breed he was: many people adore animals in general and dogs in particular.

As we turn to this mysterious and rather scary story – it could be a terrifying episode in a horror film – we're presented with a problem. Jesus drives out a legion of demons from a man who had been tormented by them for years. But there are issues: not only does Jesus negotiate with the demons rather than just expelling them, but the result of the negotiation is that a massive herd of pigs stampede down the hillside, possessed now by those same demonic spirits. They drown, a cruel death. This seems both unnecessary and harsh on the animals, but wasteful too, because this herd of swine would have been highly valuable, their loss threatening the livelihood of the hapless owner. As we'll see, the Gentile locals weren't happy at all, demanding that Jesus leave their locality, a strong reaction considering the remarkable deliverance that had taken place. A man had got his life back, but the locals didn't seem to value that. Of course, all animal cruelty is wrong. In a world where the lives of the unborn and the elderly seem increasingly threatened, do we love our pets more than people?

the
remarkable
deliverance

Prayer: Lord, may I prioritise what really matters, and live a life of love. Amen.

A hopeless situation

I've been to the place where this happened, on the far side of the Sea of Galilee. Mark gives us the most detail about the man's condition, and it's a portrait of despair and terror. Imagine a wide-eyed, screaming naked man (Luke tells us he was nude). He is charging at you, and he is much stronger than you are. His body is scarred and bloodied because, in his anguish, he has been cutting himself. Nobody had been able to subdue him – the locals had obviously tried, because his crying out and his threatening behaviour have made this place a no-go area. But a sign and a wonder is about to unfold as Jesus helps someone who has repeatedly been seen as a lost cause.

So Jesus arrives, and the utterly impossible becomes a glorious reality. Before we consider what happened, let's not lose the wonder of this, as deliverance comes, and freedom and new life is born. Perhaps you have a situation where change seems impossible. No slick slogans here, but let's affirm this together: when all else fails, God is still able.

To ponder: What 'impossible' situations do you face?

the utterly impossible
becomes a glorious reality

Whodunnit?

Read:
Mark 5:1–13
John 8:14

....

FOCUS

'*The demons begged Jesus, "Send us among the pigs; allow us to go into them."*' (Mark 5:12)

Sitting through a West End play, the tension climbed as we consider the age-old question created by a murder mystery: whodunnit? The same question needs to be asked as we see the herd of pigs gallop down the hillside to their death. First of all, remember the demons killed the pigs, not Jesus. As we'll see tomorrow, a drama is being played out here, one powerfully demonstrating the power of evil, but Jesus commanded the demons leave the man and go to the pigs, not that the pigs go charging to their own deaths. Scholars also remind us that in His earthly ministry, Jesus did not know everything, as He himself taught when asked about the details of the second coming (Mark 13:32, Matt. 24:36). So it may well be that Jesus did not anticipate the outcome of the demonic invasion of the herd. Whether that is true or not, the death of the pigs came as a result of their being under the control of the one who comes to 'steal, kill and destroy' (John 8:14).

Surely God is blamed for things for which He is not responsible, countless times every day. A person makes consistently poor choices about their diet, alcohol consumption and lack of exercise. And when they die young, others ask 'Why did the Lord take them so early?' They don't stop to think about those choices, or that all of us help determine the length of our days on earth by the way that we handle life in the here and now. Whodunnit? In the case of the hot-hoofing swine, the devil did it.

all of us help determine the length of our days

Prayer: When life goes wrong and I want quickly to find someone to blame, Lord, help me to trust in Your goodness and love. Amen.

Holiness isn't fragile

Some Christians spend their lives trying to get away from the big bad world and the influences the world brings. Interpreting the call to 'come out from among them and be separate' as a call to physical and cultural isolation, they bury themselves in Christian activities, reading Christian books, listening to so-called 'Christian' music and surrounded by... Christians! But while some relationships can be damaging and lead us astray – bad company corrupts character – Jesus shows us true holiness is not like a fragile flower, but rather is a powerful, positive force that can change those who come into contact with it. Holiness does not need to be cloistered or protected. It is able to bring wholeness where there is brokenness and scatter the forces of darkness. The demoniac was viewed as unclean for so many reasons (he lived among tombs, in Gentile territory, near swine, and was possessed by unclean spirits). Yet he is cleansed by the power of Jesus' holy presence. Likewise, the man smitten with leprosy and thus viewed as unclean was cleansed by Jesus (Mark 1:40–45). As the demons beg Jesus for permission to go into the swine, there is a powerful demonstration of what is unclean being under the dominion of the ultimately 'clean One' – the Holy Son of God Himself.

There's no such thing as a truly 'holy huddle', because holy people are called to pray for and dynamically affect those around them, and be the salt of the earth, the light of the world.

Prayer: May my life truly bring the flavour and light of Christ to my sphere of influence, Father. Amen.

Read:
Mark 5:11–12
Matthew 5:13–16

FOCUS
'The demons begged Jesus, "Send us among the pigs; allow us to go into them."' (Mark 5:12)

true holiness is...a powerful, positive force

Don't play with darkness

Read:
Mark 5:11–13
Acts 19:1–20

FOCUS
'The herd, about two thousand in number, rushed down the steep bank into the lake and were drowned.'
(Mark 5:13)

Staying in the home of an itinerant evangelist, I was surprised when he opened a cupboard filled with board games. Sitting alongside Monopoly (I love it but don't have enough years left to spend playing it), Skyjo (my favourite card game – give it a try) there sat the Ouija board. I was stunned, because that's no 'game', as people try to make contact with the spirits of the departed. Not only is that kind of activity emotionally and spiritually dangerous – I tried it in my non-Christian days – but it is also expressly forbidden in Scripture, and for good reason. My evangelist friend caught my raised eyebrow, and asked what I was anxious about, so I gently shared my concerns. He laughed, told me I was making a fuss about nothing – and never forgave me, breaking off the developing friendship there and then.

This story is a shocking drama that portrays the power of evil. The awful, tortured condition of the poor man, the effect on his wider community, and the power of destruction of the pigs we considered yesterday – all this shows us we should avoid anything to do with the occult. This is not because there's nothing in it, but because there *is* something in it, which is the power of darkness. We shouldn't be afraid of that power: the demons were afraid of Jesus, Jesus was not afraid of them. But we should be cautious and thoughtful, knowing that when it comes to the occult, there's no such thing as harmless dabbling.

there's no such thing as harmless dabbling.

Prayer: I want nothing to do with the works or power of darkness, Lord Jesus. Your power is greater, and is all I want or need. Amen.

A beautiful portrait

The gospel is about transformation. Singing, 'Amazing Grace' recently, I was reminded of the utter change that came to the author of the song, John Newton, a former slave trader. He had lived a life of utter cruelty and inhumanity: Christ transformed him completely, and he went on to fight to abolish the slave trade. The film Amazing Grace is well worth watching, to see Newton and others in action. And that process of transformation goes on, every day, all around the world. We know it does from our own lives, where we see the gospel brings beauty and change. It can be sudden, as in this case, or it can be a process over time.

As we see this man utterly restored, what a radical contrast is found in the picture. Once naked, and living with that humiliation, now he is clothed. Once insane with rage, now he is in his right mind, and can become part of his family once again.

Following Jesus means travelling a narrow road. There will be demands and self-sacrifice needed as we walk the way of discipleship. At times, the road will be steep, and the way shrouded with mystery. Our questions will not all be answered – indeed, the longer we walk with Him, perhaps the more questions emerge. But let's be clear – as we see the remarkable transformation of a tormented soul, we see and celebrate this truth: the way of Jesus is the best, the right way, life according to the Maker's design. Let's never forget that, especially when the trek is toughest.

Prayer: Lord Jesus, Your way is good, right, wholesome, true. Help me to affirm that when the road is tough or the call is demanding. Amen.

Read:
Mark 5:14–15
John 10:1–10

FOCUS

'When they came to Jesus, they saw the man who had been possessed by the legion of demons, sitting there, dressed and in his right mind.'
(Mark 5:15)

that process of transformation goes on

Christmas Eve

Read:
Luke 2:8–20
Isaiah 7:14

FOCUS

'And there were shepherds living out in the fields nearby, keeping watch over their flocks at night.'
(Luke 2:8)

Let's turn away from Gadera for the next couple of days as we celebrate Christmas. Over the last couple of months, we've considered the puzzling Jesus, and the challenge for us to allow Him to be who He truly is, rather than what we'd like Him to be. At one level, the Christmas period is perhaps the time when the greatest number of people 'revise' Jesus, turning Him into an object who appears on a greeting card. How ironic that millions will leave Him out of this time, that ostensibly celebrates His birthday. Perhaps that's why I always feel mixed emotions at Christmas; joy at the reminder of His coming to rescue us, sadness because so many choose to simply ignore the rescuer.

But with that acknowledged, consider those stunned shepherds who were treated to a glorious angelic party and the news that the Saviour of the planet had been born. What a puzzling strategy; He comes, not to kings or to crowds, not to influencers, but to a group whose testimony would not have been treated seriously, because, at that time, shepherds were thought of as rascals. The dark night sky lit up before them, their mundane shift wonderfully interrupted by the news the world had not been abandoned, and there is a God.

For all of us, the last couple of years have been shrouded in darkness and uncertainty. Pause today and tonight to celebrate this: to ordinary, often bewildered people like us, He has come to stay, as we walk with Him by His Spirit.

shepherds
were thought
of as rascals

Prayer: You are the Light of the World, Jesus. I'm grateful You have become my light, my love, my Lord. Amen.

Christmas Day

Christmas is generally thought of as a time of joy. But we should consider just why Christmas can be a time of joy, rather than just happy in a superficial sense. The Christmas message was summarised by the angels in just two words: good news – and that news leads to joy. The news was delivered to a people locked down under Roman occupation, living under harsh oppression and burdened by horrendous taxation. But news came that there was not only a God, but a God who sees, who hears our prayers and cries, who has determined to go to the most extreme lengths to intervene into human life, in the sending of His Son to live, to die, and then to be raised again to offer new life to all. This news offers direction to the bewildered, the hope of reunion to the bereaved, strength to those who are exhausted and peace to those who are troubled.

Whether you gather with family or friends today, or navigate this day alone, may You know the true joy of this day of days. And may God bless you.

To ponder: Can you think of other reasons for why the gospel, the Christian message, should be described as 'good news'?

a God who sees, who hears
our prayers and cries

Read:
Luke 2:4–10
1 Peter 1:3–8

Go away, Jesus

Read:
Mark 5:14–17
John 14:15

FOCUS

'Then the people began to plead with Jesus to leave their region.' (Mark 5:17).

The man sitting opposite me was beginning a two-day session of LifePlan coaching, where I walk a person through a series of 19 steps to evaluate where they are in their life journey and then begin to make plans for the future. He had heard I was also a pastor, and was vehement: 'Let's be clear', he said, 'I don't want to hear about any of that God stuff. My life is going well, thank you, and I don't want God to come along and mess it all up.' I assured him my coaching was not a cunning plan to convert him, but he pressed the point harder. 'NO Jesus for me!' he snorted.

As the demoniac was wonderfully restored, word gets out in the neighbourhood, and the locals gather. It's gloriously obvious a miracle has taken place. Yet there's a surprising response, as we have seen, because they immediately demand Jesus leaves their region. Perhaps their grief for the loss of the herd blinded them to the glory of seeing a man get his life back, or perhaps they hadn't cared that much in the first place. Perhaps we think we would never ask Jesus to go away, and yet it's possible, especially when we indulge in consistent disobedience, that while we don't tell Him actually to get lost, we act as if we'd like Him to. Let's continue to express our welcome to Jesus through our obedience to Him. And by the way, on the second day of our coaching, the insistent atheist said, 'Can we talk about the God stuff?' But that's another story...

our welcome to Jesus through our obedience to Him

Prayer: Lord, stay close. And enable me to see in step with You in my obedience.

What are we begging for?

Read:
Mark 5:14–19
Luke 18:1–8

I'll tell you what I want, what I really, really want, declared a certain popular girl band. And in this story, the idea of begging or pleading for something occurs no less than four times. First of all we hear the man pleading with Jesus: what do you want with me? Then the demons beg Jesus to send them into the nearby pigs. We're reminded just who it is who in charge: the powers of darkness do the begging, the Son of God does the permitting. And then the locals plead with Jesus to leave their region. This was not a mild request; they desperately want Him to be gone. It shows us that even the greatest miracle will not convince the sceptical or hardened heart. 'If I could just see it, I'd believe' is simply not true as a maxim. In our early days of ministry, a local man experienced such a stunning healing miracle after prayer that he called a live phone-in radio show and breathlessly reported what had happened to him. But as far as I know, though the healing was verified, he never came to faith. Finally, there is the beautiful sight of the restored demoniac, now pleading to be with Jesus. Mark uses language that shows he was desperate to become one of Jesus' disciples. The heart of discipleship is not just learning from or about Jesus, but being in company with Him. More of that tomorrow, but as we see a rescued soul almost frantic about being with His rescuer, I want to have a similar hunger and thirst for God.

FOCUS

'Then the people began to plead with Jesus to leave their region.' (Mark 5:17).

Prayer: Earnestly I seek you; I thirst for you, my whole being longs for you, in a dry and parched land where there is no water. Amen. (Ps 63:1).

the Son of God does the permitting

Tell/don't tell

Read:
Mark 5:18–19
Mark 3:7–12

FOCUS

'Go home to your own people and tell them how much the Lord has done for you, and how he has had mercy on you.'
(Mark 5:19)

Commentators call it the Messianic secret. It's the term used to describe Jesus' pattern of ministry, where He would perform a mighty miracle, but then instruct the person involved not to tell anyone about what had happened to them. But here, in the case of the Gadarene demoniac, Jesus orders him to share the news of his deliverance far and wide. That seems puzzling – why the secrecy on one hand and the command to share on the other? The answer is that the secretive approach was taken with the Jewish population. We've already seen they had expectations of a military Messiah, and so too much talk could provoke a premature reaction from the Roman authorities. It might even have prevented Jesus from completing His ministry, if He was executed early, with His mission not yet complete. But the Gentiles, like the former demoniac, had no such anticipation of a rescuing, military Messiah, and so they had no previous expectations to shape their view of Jesus.

Sometimes, what we feel we know of Jesus can stand in the way of fresh understanding. A new convert, hungry for truth, can be a more open book because there are no preconceptions to cloud their vision.

We all need to continue our journey of faith with open hearts, staying teachable, firm in the foundations of our faith yet willing to dialogue and discuss different shades of opinion and viewpoints, lest what we know becomes an obstacle to what we might yet learn and understand.

no pre-conceptions to cloud their vision

Prayer: Increase my vision and knowledge of You, Lord. Show me where my understanding of You and Your ways is flawed. Amen.

Stay home

Attending an ordination service for pastors who had completed their leadership training, I was taken aback by some words spoken by the preacher during that service. 'Being a pastor or a missionary is the highest calling available', he enthused. 'You are greatly privileged to be recipients of that high call.' Let me clearly say serving in teaching and leadership is indeed a wonderful privilege, and I'm so grateful for it – most of the time! But the blinkered suggestion it is the 'highest' calling disturbs me, not least because it devalues those who are called to serve in the marketplace, the home, or any other form of 'non-ministry' activity. For anyone called into business, being a pastor or missionary is not the highest calling – it's the wrong calling. And I've seen too many ministry people who were obviously not equipped to lead local churches, but stayed in place, hurting themselves and their congregations in the process, because they were reluctant to step away from the 'highest' calling. Jesus' response to the pleading of the former demoniac who so wanted to be with Him and His team shows us there is not one way to frame discipleship. In his case, the call was not to go, but to stay, and be a dynamic witness in his own locality. God has purposes written over all our lives. Let's stay in the lane of His calling for us, and not stray into thinking other pathways are more significant.

Read:
Mark 5:18–20
Matthew 28:19–20

FOCUS

'So the man went away and began to tell in the Decapolis how much Jesus had done for him.'
(Mark 5:20)

Prayer: Lead me in the way that You uniquely have for me, Lord. Save me from the perils of comparison. Amen.

God has purposes written over all our lives

What Jesus has done for me

Read:
Mark 5:1–20
Romans 1:8–17

FOCUS

'So the man went away and began to tell in the Decapolis how much Jesus had done for him. And all the people were amazed.'
(Mark 5:20)

I don't often hear the word 'evangelism' these days. In my early years as a follower of Jesus, we were rightly encouraged to share our faith at every opportunity. Gathering weekly in the youth group, we would often ask for prayer for those with whom we'd shared the good news. There was a high level of expectation that God would use our faltering conversations. We had evangelism training, some of which was useful, some of which was cheesy. At times, we felt like trainee salespeople desperately trying to push our product.

These days, we can fall silent, perhaps more nervous because sharing a message about a Jesus who claims to be uniquely the way to God is challenging in a pluralistic society. It can be awkward, and any sense of certainty frowned on as bigotry. Instead of speaking out, we hope living well for Christ will draw attention to Christ. But as we read about always being prepared to give an explanation for our hope, let's be ready to do so, realising we don't have to learn a script, or produce a slick line of patter, to be able to witness. As the former demoniac discovered, his message was simple: look what Jesus has done for me. That is the heart of our message too.

Thank you for joining me in our exploration, looking at some of the more puzzling events in the life and ministry of Jesus. May you have a new year filled with hope and joy – and opportunities to pass the good news on.

let's be ready to speak up

Prayer: In this new year, Lord, may my life and words speak powerfully of Your transforming power. Thank You for what You have done for me. Amen.

Order form

5 Easy Ways To Order

1. Visit our online store at **waverleyabbeyresources.org/store**
2. Send this form together with your payment to: **Waverley Abbey Resources, Waverley Abbey House, Waverley Lane, Farnham, Surrey GU9 8EP**
3. Phone in your credit card order: **01252 784700** (Mon–Fri, 9.30am – 4.30pm)
4. Visit a Christian bookshop
5. For Australia and New Zealand visit KI Entertainment **kigifts.com.au**

For a list of our National Distributors, who supply countries outside the UK, visit waverleyabbeyresources.org/distributors

Your Details (required for orders and donations)

Full Name:	CWR ID No. (if known):
Home Address:	
	Postcode:
Telephone No. (for queries):	Email:

Publications

TITLE	QTY	PRICE	TOTAL
		Total Publications	
UK P&P: up to £24.99 = **£2.99**; £25.00 and over = **FREE**			
Elsewhere P&P: up to £10 = **£4.95**; £10.01 – £50 = **£6.95**; £50.01 – £99.99 = **£10**; £100 and over = **£30**			
Total Publications and P&P (please allow 14 days for delivery)		**A**	

All Waverley Abbey Resources Bible Reading notes are also available as single issue **ebooks**.
Visit **waverleyabbeyresources.org** for further information.

Continued overleaf >>

How would you like to hear from us? We would love to keep you up to date on all aspects of the CWR ministry, including; new publications, events & courses as well as how you can support us.

If you **DO** want to hear from us on email, please tick here [ ]

If you **DO NOT** want us to contact you by post, please tick here [ ]

You can update your preferences at any time by contacting our customer services team on 01252 784 700. You can view our privacy policy online at waverleyabbeyresources.org

<< See previous page for start of order form

Payment Details

☐ I enclose a cheque/PO made payable to CWR for the amount of: **£** _____

☐ Please charge my credit/debit card.

Cardholder's Name (in BLOCK CAPITALS) _____

Card No. | | | | | | | | | | | | | | | | |

Expires End | | | | | Security Code | | | |

Gift to CWR   ☐ Please send me an acknowledgement of my gift   **C** [   ]

Gift Aid (your home address required, see overleaf)

giftaid it I am a UK taxpayer and want CWR to reclaim the tax on all my donations for the four years prior to this year **and on** all donations I make from the date of this Gift Aid declaration until further notice.*

Taxpayer's Full Name (in BLOCK CAPITALS) _____

Signature _____ **Date** _____

*I am a UK taxpayer and understand that if I pay less Income Tax and/or Capital Gains Tax than the amount of Gift Aid claimed on all my donations in that tax year it is my responsibility to pay any difference.

GRAND TOTAL (Total of A, B & C) [   ]

CWR Instruction to your Bank or Building Society to pay by Direct Debit

Please fill in the form and send to: CWR, Waverley Abbey House, Waverley Lane, Farnham, Surrey GU9 8EP

DIRECT Debit

Name and full postal address of your Bank or Building Society

To: The Manager _____ Bank/Building Society

Address _____

_____

_____

_____ Postcode

Name(s) of Account Holder(s)

[   ]

Branch Sort Code

| | | | | | |

Bank/Building Society Account Number

| | | | | | | | |

Originator's Identification Number

| 4 | 2 | 0 | 4 | 8 | 7 |

Reference

| | | | | | | | | | | | | | | | |

Instruction to your Bank or Building Society

Please pay CWR Direct Debits from the account detailed in this Instruct subject to the safeguards assured by the Direct Debit Guarantee. I understand that this Instruction may remain with CWR and, if so, detai will be passed electronically to my Bank/Building Society.

Signature(s)

_____

_____

Date _____

Banks and Building Societies may not accept Direct Debit Instructions for some types of account